cooking with
GOCHUJANG

cooking with
GOCHUJANG

naomi imatome-yun

THE COUNTRYMAN PRESS · WOODSTOCK · VT

Published by The Countryman Press, P.O. Box 748, Woodstock, VT 05091
Distributed by W. W. Norton & Company, Inc., 500 Fifth Avenue, New York, NY 10110
Printed in the United States of America

Cooking with Gochujang
978-58157-252-0

10 9 8 7 6 5 4 3 2 1

TO DAVID, LUCAS, ZEKE,

AND GREAT TEACHERS EVERYWHERE

contents

37 appetizers, sides, and vegetable dishes

59 soups and stews

introduction

*M*eet *gochujang,* the not-yet-famous hot sauce from Korea. I don't think you can ever have too much hot sauce in your life, so I don't think gochujang has to knock all the others off your pantry shelf. Sriracha is trendier, and I do love a good sambal or a splash of Tapatio on my eggs. You might not ever see a gochujang-themed T-shirt, but I do believe that this Korean mother sauce is the most versatile hot sauce out there.

WHAT IS GOCHUJANG?

Gochujang isn't a fiery, in-your-face hot sauce. It's a chili paste with a complex spicy, sweet, and deep flavor. The spice is not aggressive, so it's not just a hot sauce that adds some fire to your food. Instead, gochujang is a savory sauce that can give an umami boost to almost every dish.

Gochujang is thicker than other hot sauces you're probably used to; it's more of a paste with the consistency of hoisin sauce, so you can't squirt it out of a bottle. It ranges in color from a ketchup shade to a deep brick red, depending on the type and age of the gochujang. It's concentrated, so even a tablespoon can add richness and a deep flavor to a sauce, stew, or marinade.

WHAT'S IN IT?

This essential Korean sauce and condiment is made of chili peppers, soybeans, sticky rice powder, and salt. Fermentation gives the sauce its deep, rich flavor. If you're afraid of that word, *fermentation,* then just think of beer and bread. We can thank the natural fermentation process for some of the most delicious food and drinks in the world. Gochujang is to regular hot sauce as wine is to grape juice: the fermentation process adds richness, flavor, and health benefits to the original ingredients. If you're more familiar with Japanese food, then think of gochujang as a spicy, earthy miso paste. Bon Appetit describes it as "bold miso meets that stuff in the rooster bottle."

GOCHUJANG GOES GLOBAL

The Food Network blog calls gochujang "the next best thing you never ate," which is only true if you haven't eaten Korean food before. If you have, then you'll recognize the taste of gochujang from *bibimbap* (mixed rice with vegetables) or *dukboki* (spicy stir-fried rice cakes).

Gochujang is a star sauce in Korean cooking, but you can also use gochujang in a million other dishes. As with Korean cuisine in general, the possibilities are endless. The thing I love about cooking Korean food is that I can be adventurous and flexible. You don't have to stick to a recipe religiously—use a different protein or add more onions and omit green peppers if that suits you better.

Gochujang adds depth and a slow-burning heat to marinades, soups, stews, salad dressings, and even cocktails. Blend gochujang with mayo, ketchup, barbecue sauce, or ranch dressing for a great dipping sauce. Add some to marinades, vinaigrettes, and hearty stews like chili for amazing results. Gochujang can elevate everyday fare—from burger and fries to bagel with cream cheese—to extraordinary heights. Just beware, it's easy to get addicted to the stuff.

THE HISTORY OF GOCHUJANG

Korea is a nation on a small peninsula. Its mountainous terrain, distinct seasons, different coastal regions, and neighbors (China and Japan) have all influenced its cuisine. Korean cooking features advanced pickling and preserving methods, and imaginative uses of every possible food resource available to the people. One of the most incredible parts of Korean food history is that one of the defining aspects of Korean cuisine—its spiciness—is imported.

The chili pepper is native to South America. It is actually the Spanish explorer Christopher Columbus who is credited with bringing the chili pepper to Europe. From there, Portuguese traders brought the pepper to the Asian continent via India. It didn't take long for the chili to become popular all over Asia; in fact, it's impossible to imagine most Asian cuisines without some spice and heat. Whether the chili pepper made it to Japan via the Chinese or the Portuguese is unclear, but an early seventeenth-century Korean record written by scholar Yi Sugwang notes that chili peppers were brought into Korea by the Japanese.

An eighteenth-century text, the *Jungbo Sallim Geongje* (1765), contains what might be the first record of gochujang, although it was probably made earlier than that. Gochujang was first created by adding ground-up chilies to fermented soybeans with glutinous rice flour, and then fermenting the mixture in the sun in earthenware pots. Gochujang is still made with those same ingredients today.

Until recently, gochujang was made individually in every household, meaning that recipes and flavor varied among families, towns, and regions. Commercial production of gochujang took off in the 1970s, and now most gochujang does not come from family pots. When I asked friends and family in Korea for their own gochujang recipes, most of them laughed in disbelief. Even older relatives and friends revealed that they had not made their own gochujang in a very long time. In the same way that most Americans don't make ketchup and mayonnaise at home, the vast majority of people in modernized South Korea buy their gochujang from grocery stores.

Gochu means chili and *jang* means sauce in Korean. Along with *ganjang* (soy sauce) and *daenjang* (a fermented soybean paste similar to Japanese miso), gochujang is one of Korea's most essential mother sauces.

WHERE TO BUY GOCHUJANG IN AMERICA

It's easy and convenient to get gochujang in the States. Most Asian grocery stores carry it. Even if you don't live near an Asian market, you can easily order it online from places like Amazon. There are even mass market retail brands that offer Americanized versions of the sauce.

WHAT TO LOOK FOR

Gochujang is often sold commercially in red tubs of different sizes, and the label will often note whether it's a mild, medium, or spicy variety. Refrigerate it after opening and it will easily last for a year (or more) in your refrigerator.

An important thing to remember is that gochujang is sold at different spice levels and each variety tastes different, so plan to taste and adjust accordingly. The recipes in this cookbook are all based on gochujang that is at the medium spice level.

HOW TO MAKE GOCHUJANG

Even in Korea, most people don't make their own gochujang these days. But if you do make it at home the traditional way, you'll be rewarded with a deeper, richer flavored paste that will last you many months. Even if you opt for the quicker "homemade" version with miso, you'll be able to experiment to find the right balance of spicy, sweet, and salty that suits your palate.

Traditional Gochujang

This traditional recipe takes time, patience, and a sunny spot to allow your gochujang to ferment. It's a labor of love, but the end result is a rich, mellow chili paste that you can't get in a mass-produced gochujang. Commercial production often uses lower quality wheat and soy products to keep costs down or adds corn syrup to sweeten the paste, so be sure to read your labels as you shop.

 7 CUPS   **3 WEEKS**

INGREDIENTS

3/4 cup barley malt powder

2 1/2 cups water

1 cup sweet rice flour (sometimes labeled "glutinous rice flour")

1 cup *gochukaru* (Korean chili pepper powder)

1/2 cup fermented soybean powder *(meju garu)*

1/2 cup kosher salt

DIRECTIONS

Combine the malt powder and water. Stir to dissolve powder into water Strain mixture and put into a large soup pot.

Heat up on the stove for about 25 minutes, but do not boil the mixture. When it starts to simmer, turn the heat down. Remove from heat and add the sweet rice flour. Stir to combine. Cool to room temperature.

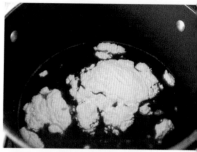

In a large bowl, combine the cooled rice and malt paste, gochukaru, soybean powder, and half of the salt. Mix to combine. Cover with a clean kitchen towel and let stand overnight. Mix again the next day.

Sprinkle half of the remaining salt onto the bottom of a glass or earthenware jar. Pour the paste into the jar.

Sprinkle the rest of the salt on top of the paste. Make sure you leave a few inches of room at the top of the container.

The traditional earthenware pots let the gochujang breathe and ferment, but you can also do this by covering the top of your glass jar with a cheesecloth or breathable fabric.

Let your gochujang sit in the sun during the day and then loosely cover at night with a lid, or bring indoors if it's cold out.

Stir the gochujang every few days.

After at least 3 weeks, your gochujang is mature enough to enjoy.

Scrape off the salt on top and stir your gochujang.

Store in the refrigerator for up to one year.

Quick Gochujang

This quick and easy nontraditional recipe yields a delicious gochujang variation. Make it when you don't have the time to source the regular ingredients needed to make the real thing.

 4 CUPS **33 MINUTES**

INGREDIENTS

2 cups white miso

1/2 cup sugar

3 Tbsp honey

3/4 cup soy sauce

1/2 cup gochukaru (Korean chili pepper powder)*

DIRECTIONS

Mix all ingredients together and warm up in a pot over low heat. Heat for 15 minutes and never let it get up to simmering. Let cool to room temperature and store in the refrigerator.

Since this is a creative and completely nontraditional recipe, you can also substitute Korean chili pepper powder for other types of red pepper powder and adjust the ingredients to your desired sweet and salty levels.

sauces, marinades, dips, and dressings

When mixing gochujang into a dipping sauce, it's easiest to work with at room temperature because it's softer and more pliable. Gochujang lasts for a very long time if kept in the refrigerator, but many people keep it on the counter for periods too. It has a naturally long shelf life due to the fermentation process and the salt, which acts as a preservative. So don't be nervous to keep it out for a few hours in advance of cooking.

With all of these sauces, dips, and dressings, how much you use depends on how spicy your gochujang is and also how spicy you like your condiments.

gochujang KETCHUP

1/4 CUP

Gochujang ketchup can be used for french fries, omelets, and anything else you can think of.

INGREDIENTS

1 Tbsp gochujang
3 Tbsp ketchup

DIRECTIONS

Mix together until blended.

korean "SPECIAL SAUCE"

Use this special sauce on burgers, sandwiches, or as a dipping sauce for chips or french fries.

 1/4 CUP

INGREDIENTS

1 Tbsp mayonnaise
1 Tbsp ketchup
1 Tbsp gochujang

DIRECTIONS

Mix the ingredients together until well blended.

YOGURT DIP

You can use this as a dip for vegetables or chips, or as a side to curry, chili, and meat dishes. Throw in some fresh herbs if you have them.

 1/2 CUP

INGREDIENTS

1/4 cup plain Greek yogurt
3 Tbsp sour cream
3 Tbsp gochujang
1 Tbsp freshly squeezed lemon juice

DIRECTIONS

Combine the ingredients in a bowl and mix together.

gochujang BUTTER

Use this butter on seafood like oysters or clams, on crusty bread, or as a seasoning mixture with Parmesan and pepper for plain pasta.

 1/2 CUP **5 MINUTES**

INGREDIENTS

1/2 stick (4 Tbsp) butter
2 tsp to 1 Tbsp gochujang

DIRECTIONS

In a small saucepan, melt down the butter over low-medium heat.

Add the desired amount of gochujang, depending on how spicy you want it.

Whisk to combine.

gochujang
MAYO

▤ **1/3 CUP**

This is a heavenly combination that you can use on french fries, hamburgers, sandwiches, vegetables, and anything else that needs a little pick-me-up. This recipe uses a basic ratio of ingredients. You can adjust it by adding chopped onions or omitting the garlic, or adjust the spice ratio to your taste. Have fun eating this up—you can use it on everything!

INGREDIENTS

1/4 cup mayonnaise
2 Tbsp gochujang
2 tsp minced garlic

DIRECTIONS

Mix all ingredients together until completely blended.

gochujang VINAIGRETTE

This is an amazing dressing for salads. I especially love to use it on soba salads and cold shrimp and chicken dishes.

 1/2 CUP **5 MINUTES**

INGREDIENTS

2 Tbsp gochujang
1 Tbsp sugar
2 Tbsp rice vinegar
1 Tbsp olive oil
1 Tbsp sesame oil
2 Tbsp soy sauce
1 clove garlic, minced

DIRECTIONS

Whisk all the ingredients together until well combined.

spicy pork
MARINADE

This marinade goes with any type of pork, from ribs and chops to grilled dishes and stir fry.

 1 1/2 CUP   **5 MINUTES**

INGREDIENTS

1 onion, minced
2 Tbsp minced garlic
1 Tbsp sesame oil
2 Tbsp soy sauce
4 Tbsp gochujang
5 Tbsp sugar
2 Tbsp rice wine
2 tsp minced ginger

DIRECTIONS

Mix ingredients together until well blended.

spicy beef MARINADE

This is the basic marinade recipe for Korean barbecued meats with the addition of gochujang for some spice. This recipe makes enough for 1 pound of meat, but I usually triple or quadruple it to keep in the fridge for use on anything from chicken to sliced steak.

 1 1/4 CUPS   **8 MINUTES**

INGREDIENTS

3 Tbsp chopped garlic (about 2 cloves)

3 Tbsp soy sauce

2 Tbsp sugar

4–5 Tbsp gochujang

1 Tbsp honey

2 Tbsp fresh-squeezed juice from an Asian pear

1 Tbsp Japanese rice wine (mirin)

1 Tbsp sesame oil

3 green onions, finely chopped (including white part)

1 tsp pepper

DIRECTIONS

Mix marinade ingredients together until sugar and honey are dissolved/distributed.

sweet and spicy
DIPPING SAUCE

This spicy-sweet chili pepper Korean dipping sauce, called *cho gochujang* or *chojang* for short, is primarily used for mixed rice dishes (bibimbap and *hwe dub bap*). It can also be used as a vegetable dipping sauce or as a spicy salad dressing. Although these are the general ingredients, everyone has different proportions of the sweet-spicy-sour flavor that they like.

This is loosely based on my sister's recipe, which is loosely based on her in-law's proportions. Her family uses it as a dipping sauce for everything, from the traditional Korean dishes to grilled chicken, eggs, and vegetables.

 3/4 CUP **5 MINUTES**

INGREDIENTS

5 Tbsp gochujang
1 Tbsp sugar
2 Tbsp honey
3 Tbsp rice wine vinegar

2 tsp minced garlic
1 tsp sesame oil
Water to thin, if necessary

DIRECTIONS

Mix all ingredients together until well blended.

If sauce consistency is too thick, thin out with some warm water.

Use immediately or store in fridge.

lettuce wrap SAUCE

Ssam jang is the special sauce that gives Korean lettuce wraps that special *pow, wow,* or *bam! Ssam bap* translates to "wrapped rice," and the wrap can be anything from lettuce leaves to thin rice paper wraps. Ssam bap is most commonly made with some sort of protein (beef, chicken, pork) with rice and a dollop of this sauce, wrapped in lettuce leaves. There's a lot of variation, so you can adjust for texture and flavor. I like mine to be spicy-sweet, full of garlic, and not too thick. If you prefer earthier flavors and less spice, then you can reverse the amount of gochujang and *daenjang* (Korean fermented soybean paste) in the recipe.

 1 1/4 CUPS   **10 MINUTES**

INGREDIENTS

1/4 cup gochujang

1/3 cup daenjang

5 cloves garlic, minced

1/4 sweet onion, minced

1 green chili pepper, chopped finely

2 green onions, chopped

2 Tbsp rice wine

1 Tbsp honey

1 Tbsp sesame oil

Black pepper to taste

Water to thin, if needed

DIRECTIONS

Mix the ingredients well.

Depending on the type of gochujang and daenjang you use, your ssam jang may be too thick. You can thin it with water or sesame oil.

This will keep in your fridge for weeks.

appetizers, sides, and vegetable dishes

saucy-spicy-sweet
TOFU

This lovely vegetarian dish will please both your vegan and your hardcore carnivore friends. The flavors are that good! This recipe makes a simple, easy weeknight dish or a delicious side to accompany a larger meal.

 4 SERVINGS   **25 MINUTES**

INGREDIENTS

1 package firm tofu, drained and sliced into
   squares or rectangles
2 Tbsp soy sauce
1 Tbsp brown sugar
1 1/2 Tbsp ketchup

1 1/2 Tbsp gochujang
1 clove garlic, minced
1 Tbsp vegetable oil (for frying)
Scallions (optional garnish)
Toasted sesame seeds (optional garnish)

DIRECTIONS

Lay out some paper towels and place your tofu squares or rectangles on top. Lay another layer on top and press lightly, trying to get all the moisture out of the tofu.

Mix all the sauce ingredients and spices together (soy sauce, sugar, ketchup, gochujang, garlic) in a wide and shallow bowl.

Place the tofu in the soy sauce mixture and soak for ten minutes.

Heat up a large skillet. Add the vegetable oil. Immediately add the tofu to the pan in one layer.

Cook on one side until the color deepens and it gets a little crispy.

Flip over and cook on the other side.

Sprinkle with some chopped scallions and/or some sesame seeds if you wish. Serve with rice.

seoulful cheese dip
TWO WAYS

This is an easy-to-whip-together dip for chips, vegetables, and crackers that always has people asking for the recipe. It's creamy with a little heat; and I've also included here a fun variation on Buffalo chicken wings for your eating pleasure.

 4-6 SERVINGS AS AN APPETIZER   **10 MINUTES**

INGREDIENTS

1 (8-oz) package of cream cheese
1/4 cup half-and-half
2 cloves garlic, minced

2 Tbsp gochujang
1 tsp fresh lemon juice
1 small sweet onion, grated

DIRECTIONS

Soften the cream cheese and stir in the half-and-half until it's creamy. Add the rest of the ingredients and mix with a fork until it reaches a smooth consistency.

For the Buffalo Wings Variation

 6 SERVINGS AS AN APPETIZER   **15 MINUTES**

INGREDIENTS

1/2 cup crumbled blue cheese
1/4 cup ranch dressing
3 Tbsp Frank's RedHot sauce

DIRECTIONS

Preheat the oven to 400°F. Add the blue cheese, ranch dressing, and Frank's RedHot sauce to the prepared Seoulful Cheese Dip. Pour into a baking dish and bake until the dip is hot and bubbly. Serve with celery sticks and cooked chicken that has been cut into strips for dipping.

oven-roasted CHICKPEAS

 1-2 SERVINGS

 30 MINUTES

These roasted chickpeas are so good that we never have any leftovers!

INGREDIENTS

1 cup cooked chickpeas (if using canned, drain and rinse)

1 Tbsp olive oil

2 tsp gochujang

Sea salt to taste

DIRECTIONS

Preheat oven to 400°F. Make sure the chickpeas are very dry. Roll or pat them down with a towel if needed. In a bowl, stir the olive oil, gochujang, and some sea salt together. Toss with the chickpeas until they are coated.

On a large baking sheet, spread out the chickpeas and roast for about 25 minutes. Halfway through, toss the pan so that the chickpeas cook on all sides.

If you want to add additional flavor, sprinkle with more sea salt, Parmesan cheese, or brown sugar after you take the chickpeas out of the oven.

cheesy spiced CORN

This is a Korean take on spicy grilled Mexican corn. Make this when sweet corn is in season and you'll be in veggie heaven.

 4 SERVINGS   **15 MINUTES**

INGREDIENTS

4 ears fresh corn
1/2 cup grated Parmesan cheese
2 Tbsp gochujang butter (see page 28)
1 lime, cut into wedges

DIRECTIONS

Grill or boil the corn for about 10 minutes.

Spread out the Parmesan on a plate.

Spread butter over each ear of corn and then roll in the Parmesan.

Serve lime wedges next to corn for squeezing.

EGGPLANT

This simple basting sauce is good on eggplants, onions, zucchini, and any other vegetables you want to throw on the fire. You'll probably have leftover sauce from this recipe, so feel free to spread it around on grilled scallions or other vegetables.

 **4 SERVINGS** **10 MINUTES**

INGREDIENTS

1 Tbsp gochujang
1 Tbsp soy sauce
1 Tbsp peanut oil
4 Asian eggplants (the small ones), cut in half

DIRECTIONS

Mix the gochujang, soy sauce, and peanut oil together.

Brush oil mixture onto both sides of eggplants.

Grill eggplants for 2–3 minutes per side, or until browned or tender.

Garnish with leftover sauce, chili peppers, scallions, or cilantro.

stir-fried
SPICED POTATOES

One of my favorite potato recipes in the world is a spicy Nepali potato dish called *aloo dum*. This is a Koreanized version of that dish that uses the technique of cooking the spices in oil before seasoning and frying the potatoes.

 4 SERVINGS   **25 MINUTES**

INGREDIENTS

1 lb potatoes, peeled and cut into bite-sized pieces

1 Tbsp sesame oil

2 Tbsp gochujang

2 tsp chili pepper powder (gochukaru)

1 garlic clove, minced

DIRECTIONS

Boil the potatoes until they are cooked and tender (about 12–15 minutes depending on the type of potatoes you use). Drain and set aside.

Heat up a large sauté pan over high heat and add sesame oil.

Add gochujang, chili pepper powder, and garlic. Mix quickly in the oil for 1–2 minutes.

Lower heat, add potatoes and pan-fry them until they are coated with the seasoning.

Take off heat.

smoky, spicy
BABAGANOUSH

I love hummus for its satisfying creaminess, but I love babaganoush when I want more smoke and noise. This is a simplified version of babaganoush with an added layer of spicy-sweet gochujang.

 8 SERVINGS AS AN APPETIZER **45 MINUTES**

INGREDIENTS

3 medium eggplants
3 cloves garlic, minced
1 lemon, juiced
1/3 cup tahini sesame paste
2–3 Tbsp gochujang (depending on the spiciness of your gochujang and the level of spiciness you want to achieve)
Sea salt
Olive oil (for roasting)

DIRECTIONS

Preheat your oven to 375°F. Prick the eggplants with a fork and char them under the broiler of your toaster oven, on your grill, or directly over the flame of your gas burner until they're charred on the outside. A few minutes is fine.

Put the eggplants on a baking sheet and roast for about 25 minutes. They should be completely soft. Remove from the oven and let them cool down enough to handle.Split the eggplants and scrape out the pulp into a bowl.

Purée the eggplant "meat" in a blender or food processor with all the other ingredients until it reaches your desired consistency. I like mine chunkier rather than very smooth.

Serve with fresh herbs, crackers, sliced bread, toasted pita chips, and/or vegetables.

grilled asparagus with
GOCHUJANG MAYO

Asparagus is always good on the grill because its texture stands up to the heat. The gochujang mayo adds just a touch of creamy spice to the dish.

 4 SERVINGS AS SIDE DISH **15 MINUTES**

INGREDIENTS

1 pound fresh asparagus spears, rinsed
   and trimmed
1 Tbsp olive oil

Salt and pepper to taste
2–3 Tbsp gochujang mayo (to drizzle) (see
   page 29)

DIRECTIONS

Preheat the grill to high.

Toss the asparagus with the olive oil.

Season with salt and pepper.

Grill over high heat for about 3 minutes, or longer if you like your asparagus on the softer side.

Drizzle liberally with gochujang mayo.

oven-roasted CABBAGE

4 SERVINGS

40 MINUTES

If you're not already a fan of cabbage, then think outside the box and try this roasted cabbage.

Roasting gives cabbage a lovely deep flavor that surprises even cabbage-haters.

INGREDIENTS

1 Tbsp olive oil

1 Tbsp gochujang

4 slices bacon, cooked and crumbled

1 head cabbage, cut into slices about 1/2 inch thick

Sea salt and pepper to taste

DIRECTIONS

Preheat the oven to 425°F.

Mix olive oil, gochujang, and bacon crumbles together.

Brush each cabbage round with seasoned oil. Top with bacon crumbles.

Sprinkle with sea salt and pepper.

Put the cabbage on a baking sheet and bake for about 25 minutes or until cabbage starts to brown.

spicy beef
SALAD

This recipe is inspired by Thai beef salad, which is my sister's favorite dish and one that has grown on me over the years. This is how I usually re-create the original with what I have in my kitchen.

 4 SERVINGS   **25 MINUTES**

INGREDIENTS

2 tsp olive oil
4 beef tenderloin steaks, trimmed
Salt and pepper to taste
2 cups hearts of romaine lettuce, cut into
   bite-sized pieces

1/2 red onion, thinly sliced
1/3 cup sliced scallions
1/3 cup mushrooms, sliced in half
1/3 to 1/2 cup gochujang vinaigrette
   dressing (see page 30)

DIRECTIONS

In a large nonstick skillet, heat oil over medium-high heat.

Season the steaks on both sides with salt and pepper. Add steaks to pan and cook 3–4 minutes on each side. Remove steaks from pan and let rest for a few minutes. When cooled, cut into thin strips.

In a large salad bowl, add the beef strips, lettuce, onions, scallions, and mushrooms.

Drizzle with gochujang vinaigrette dressing and toss.

shaved sprouts and KALE SALAD

A powerful gochujang salad dressing can stand up to the crunchy, firm textures of shaved Brussels sprouts, kale, and red cabbage. The apple adds some sweetness and the red onion and avocado add dimension to this hearty dish.

 4 SERVINGS AS A SMALL SIDE DISH   **15 MINUTES**

INGREDIENTS

1/2 pound Brussels sprouts, rinsed with tough outer leaves removed and shaved with a mandolin slicer or a very sharp knife

1 bunch of Tuscan kale, leaves removed from the stalk and thinly sliced

1 cup thinly sliced red cabbage

1/4 red onion, thinly sliced

1/4 crisp apple, cut into matchsticks

Small handful of pepitas (roasted pumpkin seeds)

1/4 cup gochujang vinaigrette (see page 30)

DIRECTIONS

Toss all the salad ingredients together.

Top with a generous amount of gochujang vinaigrette.

anytime, anything
SOBA SALAD

The spicy-sweet gochujang dressing goes perfectly with soba mixed with crunchy vegetables. This is more of a starting point than a recipe, so please be creative and use what you have in your pantry and refrigerator.

My mom and stepdad have been healthy farm-to-table cooks since before it ever became trendy, and I love having warm weather meals at their home. They just wander outside, pick what's ready to eat—lettuce, cucumbers, tomatoes, peppers, broccolini—and use them in meals. They usually throw their fresh-picked produce into their multi-grain, multi-bean bibimbap (mixed rice bowls), but I love their salads the most.

 2 SERVINGS **15 MINUTES**

INGREDIENTS

4–6 oz soba (buckwheat noodles), cooked according to package directions

1/4 cup gochujang vinaigrette (see page 30)

1 cup crunchy vegetables like sugar snap peas, red and yellow peppers, and cucumbers

2 cups leafy vegetables like kale or red leaf lettuce

1/2 cup protein, such as chickpeas, cooked chicken, or shrimp

DIRECTIONS

Toss all the salad ingredients with the gochujang vinaigrette in a bowl and enjoy.

soups and stews

gochujang STEW

The combination of both gochujang and daenjang (Korean soybean paste) makes for a hearty, full-flavored stew. You can also make this stew with almost any vegetables you have on hand, though potatoes and peppers are my favorite additions to the basics of zucchini and onion. I've also made this recipe very adaptable for vegetarians or vegans. This dish is called gochujang *chigae* in Korean (*chigae* means stew).

 4 SERVINGS   **35 MINUTES**

INGREDIENTS

3 cups soup stock—beef, seafood, or vegetarian depending on your dietary preferences or needs

1/2 onion, cut into bite-sized pieces

2 tsp minced garlic

1 medium zucchini, cut in half and lengthwise

2 Tbsp gochujang

1 tsp gochukaru (chili pepper powder)

2 Tbsp daenjang (or 2 1/2 Tbsp Japanese miso)

1 pack of tofu, cut into 1 x 1-inch squares

2 green onions, cut into 1-inch pieces

DIRECTIONS

In a soup pot, add the stock, onion, and garlic and bring to a boil over high heat.

Turn heat down to low simmer for 5 minutes, and then add the zucchini, gochujang, gochukaru, and daenjang. Make sure they dissolve well.

After 5 minutes, add the tofu and green onions and cook for another 5 minutes.

soft tofu *STEW*

Eating this bubbling hot stew of soft tofu is like being enveloped in a big, mama-bear hug. It's warm, comforting, and is an instant mood-lifter. Called *soondubu* in Korean, this is another dish that you can make personal and easily adjust to your spice level and flavor preference. My regular soondubu place in L.A. customizes every single order to spice level, broth type, and protein of choice.

In restaurants, *soondubuchigae* is served bubbling hot in traditional earthenware bowls. Raw egg is added to the stew and folded into the contents to cook from the heat within the bowl. Soft tofu stew with no spice is referred to as "white" in Korean restaurants (for the color of the stew, not the people who eat it).

Many Korean people like their soondubu with pork and kimchi, and it is a fantastic combination. But most of the time I crave it with clams, kimchi, and an anchovy base. As always, be creative with your Korean food.

 4 SERVINGS **35 MINUTES**

INGREDIENTS

1/2 lb or 1 cup beef or pork, thinly sliced

1/2 Tbsp garlic, finely chopped

1 Tbsp gochukaru (red pepper powder)

3 Tbsp sesame oil

2 cups anchovy stock, beef stock, or
   water

1 Tbsp gochujang

2 Tbsp soy sauce

3 cups uncoagulated tofu*

1 lb unshucked clams or 1 cup shucked
   clams, rinsed

2 scallions, sliced

1 egg (optional)

DIRECTIONS

In a soup pot, stir-fry the beef, garlic, and gochukaru in the sesame oil for about 5 minutes. Add the stock, gochujang, and soy sauce to the pot. Bring up to a hard simmer. Add the soft tofu and return to simmer. Add the clams and simmer until the clams are cooked (about 10 minutes), until they shrink or until the shells open (if using unshucked). Add the scallions and egg (if using) and take off heat.

* Uncoagulated tofu is usually sold in tubes, but you can use silken tofu if you can't find the really soft stuff. Just slice it into small cubes and cook as directed.

shirataki NOODLE SOUP

I made up this recipe one day for a friend who was on a low-carbohydrate diet. Tofu *shirataki* noodles are low-carb and low-calorie noodles that are good in soups and stir fries. Even if you don't care about carbs, this is one of the most forgiving recipes that makes the most of what you have in your fridge on any given day. Customize with different vegetables or proteins and noodles.

 4 SERVINGS **30 MINUTES**

INGREDIENTS

8 oz tofu shirataki (1 package), udon, or other noodles
1 cup round cabbage, chopped
2 Tbsp soy sauce
2 tsp chopped garlic
1 tsp sesame oil
2 Tbsp chili pepper flakes
4 cups water or soup stock
2 Tbsp gochujang
6 oz protein (sliced brisket, rotisserie chicken, canned tuna, or raw tofu sliced into chunks)
1 egg, beaten
Salt
1/2 scallion, chopped (optional)

DIRECTIONS

Cook the noodles according to package directions and set aside.

In a pot over medium heat, stir-fry the cabbage with the soy sauce, garlic, sesame oil, and chili pepper for a few minutes, or until the leaves begin to look transparent. Add the water and bring up to a boil. Reduce to a simmer and stir in the gochujang. Add the protein (unless you're using tofu) to the pot and wait for soup to simmer again. Slowly stream in the beaten egg. After 15 minutes, add in the noodles (and tofu, if using) and cook for 4 more minutes.

Salt to taste and garnish with scallions, if using.

spicy SHRIMP SOUP

A tasty one-pot lunch or dinner, this soup cooks in about 20 minutes and has a lovely flavor.

 4 SERVINGS　 **40 MINUTES**

INGREDIENTS

3 Tbsp wakame or Korean seaweed for soup (*miyuk*)

3 Tbsp vegetable oil

2 tsp crushed red pepper flakes

4 cloves garlic, chopped

2 Tbsp gochujang

1 inch gingerroot, peeled and cut into matchsticks

1/2 large carrot, cut into matchsticks

1 quart low-sodium chicken broth

1 pound medium shrimp, peeled and deveined

3 scallions, thinly sliced

1/2 pound vermicelli, cooked al dente (optional)

Salt and pepper to taste

DIRECTIONS

Rehydrate the seaweed for 20 minutes in a large bowl of warm water.

Heat a soup pot over medium-high heat. Add the vegetable oil, seaweed, red pepper flakes, garlic, gochujang, ginger, and carrots to pot. Sauté for 2–3 minutes. Add the chicken broth. Cover the pot and bring up to a boil. Add the shrimp and cook 3 minutes.

Lower heat, add in the scallions and noodles (if using) and cook 2 minutes, then turn off soup and let it sit a few minutes more.

Adjust flavor with salt and pepper.

spicy miso soup with
ONIONS AND POTATOES

This is a traditional way to make Japanese miso soup with some spice variety thanks to gochujang. This simple soup is mildly flavored and reminds me of my genial Japanese-Korean father who got along with everyone.

Koreans have their own version of miso called daenjang, and it's nuttier and "funkier" with more flavor. To make a Korean version of this soup, swap out 2 tablespoons of the miso for daenjang.

Just as gochujang varies in spiciness, miso varies in saltiness, so taste and adjust your seasoning accordingly.

 4 SERVINGS　 **20 MINUTES**

INGREDIENTS

3 1/2 cups dashi soup stock
1 large potato, peeled and cut into bite-sized
　chunks

1/2 onion, thinly sliced
1 1/2 Tbsp gochujang
3 Tbsp miso

DIRECTIONS

In a medium pot, heat up the dashi stock to a boil. Add the potato and onion to the pot, and simmer on medium until potatoes are soft. Add gochujang to the broth and mix to combine. Scoop out some broth from the pan into a bowl and dissolve miso into it. Pour the miso mixture into the pot and stir gently. Remove from the heat.

quick and easy
LENTIL SOUP

I love lentils as they're low in fuss and high in nutrition. They also cook pretty quickly, and lentil soup is always a heart- and belly-warming dish. This quick and spiced-up version makes a nice weeknight vegetarian dinner with a salad and some good bread.

 4 SERVINGS   **25 MINUTES**

INGREDIENTS

2 tsp olive oil

1 carrot, peeled and chopped

1 inner celery stalk, chopped

1 sweet onion, chopped

1 garlic clove, minced

Sea salt and pepper to taste

2 cups low-sodium vegetable broth

3/4 cup cooked lentils

2 heaping Tbsp of gochujang

Juice of 1/2 lemon

DIRECTIONS

In a soup pot, heat oil over medium heat. Add the carrot, celery, onion, and garlic. Season with salt and pepper and cook for 4–5 minutes. Add the broth, bring up to a boil, and simmer for 5 minutes. Add the lentils and gochujang. Stir gochujang well to distribute. Cook for 4–5 minutes. The soup will thicken. Remove from the heat and squeeze the lemon juice into the soup. Season with salt and pepper as needed.

sandwiches, wraps, and breads

bibimbap BURGER

These burgers are an East-West take on the original American favorite. This recipe is easy to replicate using other sandwich ingredients, from grilled chicken to hot dogs and grilled cheese.

 4 SERVINGS   25 MINUTES

INGREDIENTS

1/3 cup carrots, cut into matchsticks

1 Kirby cucumber, cut into matchsticks

1 tsp sea salt

3 Tbsp mayonnaise

2 Tbsp gochujang

2 tsp sesame oil

4 hamburger patties

4 sesame seed hamburger buns

2 hearts of romaine lettuce, shredded

1/2 red onion, thinly sliced

4 eggs, fried

DIRECTIONS

Season the carrots and cucumber separately with sea salt and let sit on paper towels for 10 minutes.

Combine mayonnaise and gochujang together until well combined. Set aside.

In a large sauté pan, heat the oil and cook the hamburger patties for about 4 minutes on each side for medium-rare.

Place each patty on a bottom bun, and then top with lettuce, onion, carrots, and cucumber, and a generous spoonful of gochujang mayonnaise.

Top each with a fried egg and then set the sesame bun on top.

LA-STYLE
chicken quesadillas

I count myself lucky to live in place with some of the best Korean, Korean-American, Mexican, and Mexican-American food in the States. And I'm going to go out on a limb and say that Los Angeles probably also has the best Korean-Mexican fusion food in the whole country.

 4 SERVINGS **17 MINUTES**

INGREDIENTS

3 Tbsp gochujang

4 Tbsp soy sauce

4 Tbsp rice wine

2 Tbsp honey

2 pounds skinless and boneless chicken
   thighs

6–8 tortillas, 7–8 inches

2 cups shredded cheese, Monterey Jack or
   Mexican blends work well

DIRECTIONS

For the Chicken

Mix the gochujang, soy sauce, rice wine, and honey together. In a large bowl, toss the chicken with the marinade until well coated. Let marinate at least 6 hours. Preheat the oven to 375°F. Place the chicken pieces on a baking sheet and bake for 30 minutes. Cool the chicken until you can handle it, and then chop into thin strips.

For the Quesadillas

On a flat surface, place one tortilla down and top with some shredded cheese. Top with some cooked chicken and top that with more cheese. Place a tortilla on top. Cook in a heated skillet on medium until cheese is melted. Cut into pieces and serve with gochujang yogurt dip (see page 26) and salsa.

smoked salmon "pizza" TWO WAYS

This smoked salmon flatbread is an easy appetizer because you aren't making a pie crust from scratch. Here are two ways to make this—a fresh version and a fully cooked version. The fully cooked version has more heat.

 2 SERVINGS AS AN APPETIZER **15 MINUTES**

INGREDIENTS

1 9 x 12-inch lavash (flatbread)

Olive oil, for brushing

2 Tbsp whipped cream cheese

2 Tbsp gochujang, room temperature

1 tsp fresh dill, removed from stems

1 tomato, sliced

4 ounces thinly sliced smoked salmon

1/2 red onion, thinly sliced

Small handful of dill leaves on stems

Fresh pepper to taste

DIRECTIONS

For the Fully Cooked Version

Preheat oven to 375°F. Brush the lavash with olive oil on both sides. Combine the cream cheese and gochujang together. Spread the cream cheese mixture on top of the lavash. Layer the tomato, smoked salmon, onions, and dill stems on top.

Bake for about 4–5 minutes, or until the sides of the lavash start to turn golden. Don't bake too long or the crust will become too brittle. Season with fresh pepper to taste.

For the Fresh Version

Preheat oven to 375°F. Heat the lavash up in the oven for 3–4 minutes, until the sides of the lavash start to turn golden. Combine the cream cheese and gochujang together. Set aside.

Remove the lavash from oven and brush the top with olive oil. Spread the cream cheese mixture on top. Layer the tomato, smoked salmon, onion, and dill stems on top. Sprinkle fresh pepper on top.

partytime PULL-APART BREAD

This show-stopping cheesy bread is fun and simple to make, but the gochujang butter makes it a litt
more grown-up than your standard grilled cheese or garlic bread. Perfect for parties but you could
easily make it for a great party of one.

 4 SERVINGS **40 MINUTES**

INGREDIENTS

1 loaf of good bread, sourdough works well
2 cups shredded cheese
2 Tbsp gochujang butter (see page 28)
Garlic, scallions, or chives (optional)

DIRECTIONS

Preheat oven to 350°F.

Cut the bread into a grid pattern creating 1-inch squares, making sure not to cut
through to the bottom.

Spread gochujang butter and cheese into every crevice. You don't have to be neat.
If there's any leftover butter, spread it over the top of the loaf. Cover the entire loaf
with foil.

Bake in the oven for about 15 minutes, then uncover and bake for another 10
minutes.

Pull pieces of bread off the loaf and enjoy.

easy PORK BUNS

This is a modern take on Chinese street food, and it's so delicious you'll wonder why you're not eating this every day of your life. You can buy pork buns in Asian grocery stores (fresh or frozen) or you can make them yourself—it's a basic bread recipe, but the ingredients are steamed, not baked.

 8 SERVINGS   **1 HOUR 15 MINUTES**

INGREDIENTS

For the Quick Pickled Cucumber
1 Kirby cucumber, sliced
2 tsp sugar
2 tsp sea salt

For the Quick Pickled Radish
10 red radishes, sliced into strips
2 tsp sugar
2 tsp sea salt
2 tsp white vinegar

For the Buns
1/4 cup quick pickled cucumber
1/4 cup quick pickled radish (see recipe)
8 frozen or fresh pork buns, steamed according to package directions
2 lbs pork, cut into bite-sized pieces and marinated for 1 hour in spicy pork gochujang marinade (see page31)
3 Tbsp cho gochujang sauce
4 leaves red leaf lettuce, cut into bite-sized pieces

DIRECTIONS

Sprinkle the cucumber slices with the sugar and sea salt and toss. Let sit for 10 minutes and mix again. Sprinkle the radish strips with the sugar, sea salt, and white vinegar and toss. Let stand for 10 minutes and mix again before serving.

After steaming, open the buns. If using the unsliced round buns, slice them open. At the same time as you are steaming the bread, stir-fry the pork until it is cooked (about 3–5 minutes). Spread cho gochujang sauce on the inside of each bun. Arrange the lettuce, pork, pickled radish, and pickled cucumber inside and fold closed.

rice,
noodles,
and
pasta

mixed rice bowl with
VEGETABLES (BIBIMBAP)

Bibimbap is a staple Korean rice dish that you can modify and tweak to your own palate. In restaurants, *gopdol bibimbap* is served in a piping-hot stone bowl, but at home you can also enjoy bibimbap with warm or room-temperature rice. It's gorgeous with an array of different-colored vegetables, and you can plump it up with the addition of meat, seafood, or tofu. Vegans can omit the egg if needed.

Feel free to modify the vegetables you use—get creative and use what's in season, what you discover at your local farmer's market, or even what you find in your crisper drawer. The traditional Korean way is to parboil or sauté the different colored vegetables separately, but I often add raw ingredients for some crisper textures and fresher flavors.

 4 SERVINGS   **1 HOUR**

INGREDIENTS

2 cups medium-grain rice (might be labeled as sushi rice)

1 tsp salt

1 large cucumber, julienned

1 1/2 cups bean sprouts, parboiled and squeezed of excess water

2 Tbsp sesame oil

2 carrots, julienned

4 Shiitake mushrooms, rehydrated if dried and then sliced

1 zucchini, sliced into thin strips

Sesame seeds

1/3 cup cho gochujang sauce (see recipe)

Meat or seafood (optional)

Fish eggs (optional topping)

Sesame seeds (optional)

4 eggs, fried (optional)

For the Cho Gochujang

1/4 cup gochujang

2 tsp rice wine vinegar

1 Tbsp honey

3 tsp sesame oil

1 clove garlic, minced

DIRECTIONS

For the Cho Gochujang, mix all ingredients together. The consistency of this sauce should be similar to ketchup. Just add a couple teaspoons of water if yours is too thick.

Start cooking the rice according to your rice cooker or package directions. While the rice is cooking: Dash salt sparingly on cucumber and leave to drain in a colander. After 20 minutes, squeeze out excess water from cucumber strips. Season the bean sprouts with 1 tsp of the sesame oil and salt. Sauté the carrots with a dash of salt. Sauté the mushrooms with a dash of salt. Sauté the zucchini with a dash of salt. Place the cooked rice in four separate bowls and arrange the vegetables on top. If desired, top with beef, fish eggs, sesame seeds, or a fried egg in the center. Serve each rice bowl with cho gochujang and rest of sesame oil. To eat, add a small amount of oil and desired amount of cho gochujang to your bowl and mix everything together with a spoon.

This dish, *bibim gooksu*, is the noodle version of bibimbap. These spicy cold noodles are refreshing in the summer when you don't want to spend a lot of time in front of the stove and the weather's too warm for hot, heavy dishes. It's an easy dish to throw together, but it is still full of spice, flavor, and texture and it makes for a complete and satisfying meal.

I like to make this with buckwheat noodles (*memil gooksu* or soba) since they're so delicious and healthy, but you can substitute other thin noodles if you don't have any soba at home. Try it with *naengmyun*, Korean noodles that are slightly chewy and made up of buckwheat and other flours. This is an adaptable, delicious recipe that can go a hundred different ways.

 4 SERVINGS **25 MINUTES**

INGREDIENTS

For the Gochujang Sauce

3 Tbsp gochujang
1 Tbsp soy sauce
3 Tbsp rice vinegar
1 1/2 Tbsp sesame oil

2 Tbsp honey
1 Tbsp brown sugar
1 tsp gochukaru (Korean red chili pepper powder)
1 Tbsp toasted sesame seeds

For the Noodles

10 ounces buckwheat noodles (memil gooksu, soba, about 3 bundles) or naengmyun noodles
1 small cucumber, julienned
1 cup beef or chicken, cooked and thinly sliced

1 cup kimchi, cut into small pieces
2 or 3 hard boiled eggs, sliced
3/4 cup gochujang sauce (see recipe)

Suggested Optional Toppings

1/2 carrot, julienned
5 or 6 large leaves of red leaf and/or green leaf lettuce, cut into thin strips
Asian pear, thinly sliced

Thin strips of Korean pickled radish
Korean chives or scallions
Bean or snow pea sprouts, blanched

DIRECTIONS

For the Gochujang sauce, mix everything together until well blended.

Boil water and cook the noodles according to package directions. Drain and thoroughly rinse in cold water, making sure all noodles are cool to the touch. Place noodles in 4 individual bowls, splitting all of the toppings equally. Add a dollop of the gochujang sauce to the top or leave on the side.

cold noodles with GOCHUJANG SAUCE

kimchi FRIED RICE

Kimchi bokumbap (or *bokkeumbap*) is a hearty dish that is mostly enjoyed at home, but you might also see it in some casual Korean cafes and eateries. For home cooks, it's a good way to use leftover kimchi that's past its prime. Quick, easy, and delicious, kimchi fried rice is Korean homecooking at its best.

 4 SERVINGS **35 MINUTES**

INGREDIENTS

1/3 cup thinly sliced beef, Spam, pork, bacon, or ham

1 tsp vegetable oil

1 cup Napa cabbage kimchi, chopped with any juice reserved

1/2 sweet onion, chopped

2 Tbsp gochujang

1 Tbsp finely chopped garlic

1 Tbsp soy sauce

1 Tbsp butter

3 cups cooked rice

Salt to taste

1 fried egg for each serving

DIRECTIONS

If you are using American bacon, cook the sliced bacon in an ungreased large pan and omit the oil from the next step.

With Canadian bacon, any other meat, or a vegetarian version, start here:

In a lightly oiled large pan, sauté the kimchi and onion over medium heat for a few minutes. When the vegetables begin to look transparent, add any reserved kimchi juice, the gochujang, garlic, soy sauce, and half of the butter to the pan. Sauté for another 2–3 minutes. Add the meat and continue to sauté until the meat is cooked. Turn the heat off but keep the pan on the burner. Add the remaining butter to the mix and then add in the rice (and the American bacon, if used). Mix everything to combine. Salt to taste and top with a fried egg to serve.

sweet potato noodles
WITH VEGETABLES

Chapchae (or *japchae*) is one of the most popular noodle dishes in Korea, and also seems to be one of the most popular amongst non-Koreans. The foundation of the dish is the mixture of the noodles, soy sauce, garlic, and sesame oil. The traditional version is not spicy, but my husband frequently adds a good dose of Sriracha or gochujang to ours when we eat it at home for a little kick.

Because sweet potato noodles absorb a lot of flavor, you can mix and match the vegetables or meat to your liking. I used cabbage, eggs, scallions, and onion for the version pictured here and that flavor and color combination is easy to make and tasty to eat. I have also included here a note for the more traditional version.

 4 SERVINGS   **1 HOUR 10 MINUTES**

INGREDIENTS

8 oz noodles made from sweet potato (might be called *dangmyun*, cellophane, glass noodles, or Chinese vermicelli on the packaging)

2 Tbsp vegetable or olive oil

1 sweet onion, sliced into thin strips

2 cloves garlic, finely chopped

3 scallions, chopped

1/2 cup chopped Napa cabbage

3 Tbsp soy sauce

2 Tbsp gochujang

1 tsp sugar

2 Tbsp sesame oil

Salt to taste

Sesame seeds (optional)

DIRECTIONS

Cook the noodles according to package directions. In a large wok or pan, heat the vegetable oil over medium heat. Add the onion and garlic and sauté for 1 minute. Add the scallions and cabbage and cook for 4–5 minutes, until the vegetables are almost cooked through. Turn down the heat to low and add the soy sauce, gochujang, sugar, and sesame oil. Toss in the cooked noodles and mix to combine, cooking for another 2 minutes. Top with sesame seeds, if using.

Traditional chapchae usually includes spinach, carrots, Shiitake mushrooms, and meat (beef, pork, or chicken).

creamy, spicy PASTA

This is a lip-smacking weeknight pasta recipe with quite a bit of spice. My children love this dish but always need to have a lot of water on hand!

 4 SERVINGS   **30 MINUTES**

INGREDIENTS

2 Tbsp olive oil

1 sweet onion, chopped

3 cloves garlic, minced

1 lb ground turkey

3–4 Tbsp gochujang (depending on how spicy you want it)

4 Tbsp cream cheese

1/3 cup half-and-half

Sea salt and pepper to taste

2 Tbsp chopped basil

1 lb pasta, cooked according to package directions

DIRECTIONS

Heat the olive oil in a large skillet on medium heat.

Add the onions and cook for a couple minutes. Add the garlic and cook for 1–2 minutes more.

Add the ground turkey and brown for 3–4 minutes.

Pour in the gochujang and cook for another 2–3 minutes.

Once the turkey is cooked through, add the cream cheese and half–and-half and mix to combine.

Taste and add salt, pepper, and gochujang to desired flavor.

Stir in the basil. Serve on top of pasta of your choice.

pasta with tomato, pork, and GOCHUJANG SAUCE

This is a more traditional tomato-based recipe for a meaty pasta sauce with an extra kick courtesy of a couple dollops of gochujang.

 4 SERVINGS   **30 MINUTES**

INGREDIENTS

3/4 cup ground pork

3/4 sweet onion, chopped

3 garlic cloves, minced

2 Tbsp gochujang

1 cup plain tomato sauce

1/4 cup shredded Parmesan cheese

16 oz box of spaghetti or linguine, cooked
according to package directions

Grated Parmesan (for topping)

Salt and pepper to taste

DIRECTIONS

In a large pan, cook the pork and onions over medium heat.

When the pork is almost cooked through (about 5 minutes), add the garlic.

Add the gochujang and mix the ingredients together.

Cook for a couple more minutes until combined, and then add the tomato sauce.

Heat through until the tomato sauce starts bubbling and immediately turn down heat.

Serve the sauce over pasta noodles. Add Parmesan cheese and taste. Add salt and pepper as needed.

beef,
chicken,
and pork
dishes

This recipe is easily adjusted for different levels of spiciness. For a less spicy dish, you can use just 1 Tbsp of pepper paste and no pepper flakes.

chicken and potato
STEW

This Korean stew is simple and easy to make with very little hands-on time. Simmering makes the chicken incredibly tender and the sauce adds a spicy kick. You'd probably never order this in a restaurant, but it's an example of Korean home cooking at its best. Serve it over white rice with an extra scoop of sauce for an easy and comforting meal.

 4 SERVINGS **50 MINUTES**

INGREDIENTS

2 pounds chicken thighs cut into large
   pieces
1 large carrot, peeled and cut into 2-inch
   pieces
2 onions, cut into large chunks
2 large potatoes, peeled and cut into large
   chunks

4 cloves garlic, finely chopped
2/3 cup soy sauce
1/3 cup water
3 Tbsp gochujang
1 Tbsp red pepper flakes (gochukaru)

DIRECTIONS

In a large pot over medium-high heat, combine the chicken, carrots, onions, and potatoes.

In a mixing bowl, combine the garlic, soy sauce, water, gochujang, and red pepper flakes.

Pour the mixture over the chicken and vegetables, and then bring everything to a boil.

Reduce heat to low and simmer for about 35 minutes, until sauce has thickened and chicken is cooked through.

succulent spicy PORK RIBS

These ribs are sweet, spicy, and delicious. They require some advance marinade preparation, but the waiting time is worth it. And after seasoning, they're easily cooked on the grill or in the broiler. This marinade is sweet, spicy, and is actually good for making any type of pork dish.

 4 SERVINGS   **6-12 HOURS**

INGREDIENTS

1 onion, minced

2 Tbsp minced garlic

1 Tbsp sesame oil

2 Tbsp soy sauce

4 Tbsp gochujang

5 Tbsp sugar

2 Tbsp rice wine

2 tsp minced ginger

3 lbs pork ribs, baby back or spare*

DIRECTIONS

Mix all the marinade ingredients (everything except the ribs) together until well blended.

If the ribs are not separated, cut between the bones.

Toss well to coat the ribs with marinade.

Cover and refrigerate for at least 6 hours (10–12 hours is optimal).

Grill over medium-high heat for 6–8 minutes per side. If you are cooking the ribs in the oven, broil in a 350°F oven for about an hour, turning once.

Baby back or spare ribs are best, but you can also use country-style ribs if you trim the fat.

spicy GINGER PORK

There are many people who go on and on about how perfectly gochujang complements pork. I do agree that gochujang goes well with pork—but I also think those people tend to really love pork in general—because gochujang also goes well with seafood, vegetables, and even cheese! Regardless, this tasty gochujang and ginger pork recipe is one of my favorites to serve over rice or in lettuce cups.

 3 SERVINGS **50 MINUTES**

INGREDIENTS

2 Tbsp gochujang

1 Tbsp daenjang (fermented Korean
   soybean paste) or miso

1 Tbsp honey

1 tsp grated fresh ginger

1 Tbsp soy sauce

1 onion, minced

2 garlic cloves, minced

1 Tbsp mirin

1 lb pork loin, cut into thin strips

DIRECTIONS

In a large mixing bowl, combine all the marinade ingredients (everything except the pork) together and mix well.

Add the pork and stir to coat all of pork with marinade.

Marinate for at least 30 minutes.

Heat up a griddle pan, wok, or heavy sauté pan over high heat.

Turn down heat to medium-high and add marinated pork.

Flip or turn the pork regularly and cook until pork is fully cooked and is not pink inside.

Serve in lettuce wraps or with vegetables over rice.

good grilled FLANK STEAK

I love a good marinated flank steak because it's so versatile—once it's thinly sliced, you can slide it into tacos, steak sandwiches, or lettuce wraps and use it as the protein in a beautiful salad (think romaine, blue cheese, and avocado). This is a simple recipe that you should double or triple if you are planning to serve a crowd—I never have leftovers, no matter how much I wish for them.

 **4 SERVINGS**   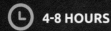 **4-8 HOURS**

INGREDIENTS

1/3 cup soy sauce

2 Tbsp honey

2 Tbsp gochujang

2–3 slices of peeled Asian pear, puréed or mashed well

2 Tbsp sesame oil

2 Tbsp minced garlic

1 1/2 lbs flank steak

Roasted sesame seeds (optional garnish)

DIRECTIONS

Combine all seasoning ingredients together (soy, honey, gochujang, pear purée, sesame oil, and garlic) in a bowl. Whisk to combine.

Place the marinade and steak in a Ziploc bag and refrigerator for 4–8 hours.

Grill the steak on a high heat for 3–5 minutes per side. Try to turn only once.

Allow the flank steak to rest for a few minutes before slicing.

Serve with rice, in salads, sandwiches, tacos, or any other way you wish.

beer-marinated CHICKEN DRUMSTICKS

This is a super-simple recipe with only five ingredients. Done on the grill, it's a no-mess, delicious dish that we sometimes serve at barbecues and summer picnics. It's also easy to double, triple, and even quadruple for group gatherings like Superbowl parties or Fourth of July celebrations.

 4 SERVINGS   **12 HOURS**

INGREDIENTS

3/4 cup of beer
3 Tbsp gochujang
Juice of one lime
1/3 cup olive oil
10 chicken drumsticks

DIRECTIONS

Mix together all of the marinade ingredients (everything except the chicken) in a mixing bowl. You might have to use a whisk to incorporate the gochujang into the beer and oil.

Place the marinade and chicken in large Ziploc bags and marinate overnight.

On a hot oiled grill, grill the chicken drumsticks for about 35–40 minutes, basting with the remaining marinade once or twice while turning.

Serve with lime slices and beer.

spicy sauced MEATBALLS

These delicious meatballs are sweet, spicy, and filling. You can serve them with pasta for an East-West version of spaghetti and meatballs, offer them up to guests as a party appetizer, or just pair them with rice and vegetables.

 **4 SERVINGS**    **30 MINUTES**

INGREDIENTS

For the Meatballs

2 lbs ground pork or ground beef or a combination of the two

3 garlic cloves, minced

2 eggs, lightly beaten

2 tsp sesame oil

1 cup Panko breadcrumbs

2 generous Tbsp of gochujang

1/2 sweet onion, finely chopped

Toasted sesame seeds (optional garnish)

Sliced scallions (optional garnish)

For the Sauce

2 Tbsp soy sauce

2 Tbsp gochujang

3 Tbsp hoisin sauce

5 Tbsp rice vinegar

2 tsp sesame oil

DIRECTIONS

Preheat your oven to 400°F.

In a large bowl, combine all meatball ingredients together gently until combined. Shape into balls the size of golf balls. Spread out the meatballs onto a greased baking sheet. You'll probably need two, depending on the size of your sheets. Bake for 10–15 minutes, or until the meatballs are brown on the outside and cooked in the center.

While the meatballs are cooking, combine all the sauce ingredients together in a sauce pot. Heat up for about 5 minutes on the stove. When meatballs are done, either brush them with sauce or coat with sauce in a large bowl. Sprinkle with optional garnish.

amazing CHICKEN WINGS

It's impossible to eat just one of these juicy, spicy, and sweet little suckers. Use these as an appetizer, main dish, or picnic dish to share. These are simple to prepare but are such crowd-pleasers that they're good for both dinner parties and casual backyard get-togethers.

 4 SERVINGS AS AN APPETIZER **2-4 HOURS**

INGREDIENTS

2 pounds chicken wings and drumettes
1-inch piece of fresh ginger, minced
1 Tbsp red pepper paste (gochujang)
2 tsp sesame oil
6 Tbsp soy sauce
3 Tbsp sugar
3 Tbsp honey
5 cloves garlic, minced
1/2 sweet onion, minced

DIRECTIONS

Mix everything but the chicken together to make the sauce. Marinate the chicken for at least an hour in the sauce (a few hours is better).

Preheat your oven to 400°F. In a heated pan on the stove, brown the chicken on all sides and reserve the marinade sauce for later. Transfer the chicken to a shallow roasting pan and pour the sauce over the pieces. Put the chicken into the preheated oven.

Turn once during cooking, covering with more sauce if needed.

Cook chicken for a total of 40–50 minutes in the oven.

grilled chicken
WITH LIME

It only takes a handful of simple ingredients to make this moist and colorful chicken dish. The sweet and savory marinade has the perfect balance of spice and sweetness.

 4 SERVINGS　 **2 HOURS 15 MINUTES**

INGREDIENTS

4 chicken thighs or breasts
4 Tbsp gochujang
2 tsp sesame oil
1 Tbsp soy sauce
2 Tbsp honey
2 Tbsp fresh lime juice

DIRECTIONS

Mix all the ingredients together, except the chicken, to make the marinade sauce.

Marinate the chicken for at least 2 hours in the sauce.

Grill the chicken for about 7 minutes per side, or until completely cooked through.

seafood

mixed rice bowl with sashimi
(HWE DUB BAP)

Hwe dub bap is a half salad and half rice bowl that combines three things Koreans love: raw seafood, rice, and spicy sauces. It is very similar to bibimbap, except that the focus is on raw for both the vegetables and the fish. The gochujang sauce in hwe dub bap is served on the side, like with bibimbap, so everyone can dress up their big bowl of sushi-grade raw fish, vegetables, and rice to their personal spice levels.

I usually like to have tuna, yellowtail, and red snapper in my hwe dub bap, but I know some people really like to have just salmon. Like most other Korean dishes, you can vary the fish and vegetables to what's fresh at the market and what you're in the mood for. Have fun using different combinations and making it as colorful as possible.

 5 SERVINGS **40 MINUTES**

INGREDIENTS

For the Gochujang Sauce (Cho Gochujang)

5 Tbsp gochujang

1 Tbsp sugar

2 Tbsp honey

3 Tbsp rice wine vinegar

2 tsp minced garlic

1 tsp sesame oil

For the Rice Bowl

5 cups cooked rice

1 head red leaf lettuce, chopped

1 small cucumber, thinly sliced

1 small carrot, julienned

7 or 8 perilla leaves, sliced thinly

2 lbs sushi-grade fish, cut into 1/2-inch to 1-inch pieces (red snapper, yellowtail, tuna, striped bass, etc.)

1 Asian pear, thinly sliced

1 cup cho gochujang (seasoned chili pepper paste), see recipe

Sesame seeds (optional garnish)

Roasted seaweed, thinly sliced (optional garnish)

Flying fish roe or pollack eggs (optional garnish)

DIRECTIONS

Mix all the gochujang sauce ingredients together until well-combined.

Divide rice into 5 bowls. Arrange vegetables, perilla leaves, fish, and sliced pear on top of rice. If using garnish, dust with sesame seeds and sliced seaweed and then top with fish eggs. Serve with small bowls of gochujang sauce on the side. To eat, mix fish, rice, and vegetables together with a generous amount of gochujang sauce to coat.

seared and glazed
SCALLOPS

Fresh scallops are so good, and these glazed and meaty morsels are divine over lentils, with soba salad, or next to some new rice. With scallops, try to get the freshest ones possible and be careful not to overcook them.

 2 SERVINGS   **20 MINUTES**

INGREDIENTS

1/2 pound large sea scallops

Salt and pepper, to taste

1 tsp gochujang

1 tsp soy sauce

2 tsp rice wine vinegar

2 tsp maple syrup

2 tsp orange juice

1 tsp sesame oil

2 garlic cloves, minced

2 Tbsp coconut oil

1/2 of a lemon, for squeezing

Cilantro, sesame seeds, scallions (optional garnishes)

DIRECTIONS

Pat the scallops dry with a paper towel to insure a nice crust. Season the scallops generously with salt and pepper. Mix together gochujang, soy sauce, vinegar, syrup, orange juice, sesame oil, and garlic in a bowl. Set aside.

Heat the coconut oil in a large pan on high heat. Just before the oil approaches the smoking point, gently place the scallops in pan. Don't overcrowd. Reduce heat to medium-low and sear the scallops for about 2 minutes until golden at the bottom.

Pour the gochujang mixture into the pan and turn scallops gently, cooking for about 2 more minutes. Remove scallops from pan and place on separate plates or serving platter. Reduce the sauce a few more minutes until it reaches a thicker glaze consistency. Drizzle sauce over the seared scallops and spritz with a squeeze of fresh lemon juice. Serve with salad, noodles, or rice.

steamy spiced
MUSSELS

These kicked-up mussels are ready in no time, and the broth is good with everything, whether you're serving rice, fresh baguettes, pasta, or french fries on the side.

 4 SERVINGS   **30 MINUTES**

INGREDIENTS

1/4 cup of gochujang
2 Tbsp minced fresh ginger
2 Tbsp sherry vinegar
6 garlic cloves, sliced
4 lbs mussels
1 tsp salt
1/4 cup olive oil
2 shallots, sliced
1 cup beer
1/2 cup sake
2 cups cooked linguine (optional)
Scallions (optional garnish)

DIRECTIONS

Combine the gochujang paste, ginger, vinegar, and garlic in a large bowl, and then set aside.

Clean your mussels by rinsing them off, submerging them in a bowl of saltwater (1 tsp will do), and then scrubbing them with a brush.

Heat up a large pot. Add the oil to the pot and cook the mussels and shallots for a couple minutes. Add the beer, cover, and cook for 1–2 minutes. Add the sake, cover the pot, and steam until the mussels open, about 4–5 minutes. Discard any mussels that are still closed. Push the mussels to one side and then add the gochujang mixture. Stir the gochujang mixture with the broth at the bottom of the pot. Carefully toss together the mussels and the sauce. If serving with noodles, separate noodles or pasta into separate bowls. Ladle out mussels and broth into individual bowls. Garnish with scallions, if using.

deconstructed spicy
TUNA ROLL

Koreans have been eating lettuce wraps since way before they became trendy in other parts of the world. They usually enjoy ssam bap ("wrapped rice") with Korean barbecue. The rice and grilled beef, pork, or chicken is combined with some gochujang sauce and rice, and then wrapped in a lettuce leaf.

This recipe is a fun take on both ssam bap and a spicy tuna roll. It's a deconstructed spicy tuna roll that diners can reconstruct into a lettuce wrap.

 2 SERVINGS AS A LIGHT APPETIZER **35 MINUTES**

INGREDIENTS

1/2 cup sushi-grade tuna, sliced or ground

2 tsp mayonnaise

2 tsp sesame oil, plus a splash

3 tsp gochujang

1 1/2 cups white rice, cooked

Furikake seasoning, as needed

Small red leaf and butter lettuce cups, washed and dried

1 scallion, sliced

1/2 sheet of nori, cut into strips

1 avocado, diced

Soy sauce (serve on the side)

DIRECTIONS

Season the tuna with the mayo, 2 tsp sesame oil, and gochujang. Mix gently to combine.

Season the rice with a splash of sesame oil and furikake seasoning.

Shape the seasoned rice into about 7–10 balls.

Plate the tuna with rice balls, lettuce, scallion, nori, and avocado so that people can make their own lettuce wraps.

reconstructed spicy
TUNA ROLL

Just like the deconstructed tuna rolll (see page 119), this tuna tower take is a re-creation of the elements of a spicy tuna rol.

 1 SERVING AS AN APPETIZER   **25 MINUTES**

INGREDIENTS

1/2 cup sushi-grade tuna, sliced or ground

2 tsp mayonnaise

2 tsp sesame oil, plus a splash

3 tsp gochujang

1 1/2 cups white rice, cooked

Furikake seasoning, as needed

1 avocado, diced

1/2 sheet of nori, cut into strips (optional garnish)

1 scallion, sliced (optional garnish)

Soy sauce (serve on the side)

DIRECTIONS

Season the tuna with the mayo, sesame oil, and gochujang. Mix gently to combine. Season the rice with a splash of sesame oil and furikake seasoning. Form the rice into a patty shape. Top with a layer of avocado. Place the seasoned tuna on top of avocado. .Garnish with nori and scallion, if using. Serve with soy sauce on the side.

broiled or grilled salmon with
SOY HONEY GLAZE

This sweet-spicy glaze works well on salmon and other meaty fishes. You can grill or broil this salmon. My mother-in-law, who is a great cook, often serves broiled fish as a side dish to meals. She cooks the fish in the toaster oven, which is a technique I've also adopted, because it is an easy way to make smaller quantities of broiled fish.

 4 SERVINGS   **20 MINUTES**

INGREDIENTS

For Soy Honey Glaze
1/3 cup soy sauce
1/3 cup sugar
2 Tbsp gochujang
2 Tbsp honey
1 tsp olive oil

For the Salmon
1 lb salmon (fillets or steaks)
5 Tbsp soy honey glaze (see recipe)

DIRECTIONS

For the glaze, mix ingredients together until well combined.

If broiling your salmon, preheat the broiler and coat the pan with oil or cooking spray. Brush the soy honey glaze on your salmon and let stand for 10–15 minutes. Place the salmon with skin side down, and brush remaining sauce over fish. Broil the salmon on the top rack for 6–8 minutes.

If grilling the salmon, grill it about 5 minutes on each side.

HALIBUT TERIYAKI

This fusion teriyaki recipe is delicious and easy when made with halibut, but also feel free to substitute striped bass, salmon, or other fish. You can also use this sauce as a base for chicken or tofu dishes.

 4 SERVINGS

INGREDIENTS

4 (4–6 oz) halibut fish fillets

2 Tbsp sake

5 Tbsp mirin (sweet cooking wine)

2 Tbsp soy sauce

2 Tbsp gochujang

2 tsp sugar

1 Tbsp canola or coconut oil for cooking

DIRECTIONS

Make the kicked-up teriyaki sauce by mixing together the sake, mirin, soy sauce, gochujang, and sugar until well blended. Using half the teriyaki sauce, marinate the fish for 5–10 minutes.

In a large sauté pan, heat the oil over medium heat. Put the marinated fish in the pan and cook for 4–5 minutes. Turn the fish over and cook for another 1–2 minutes until cooked through.

Remove fish from pan. Pour the rest of reserved marinade into pan and heat over high heat.

Bring the sauce up to a boil, reduce to simmer, and cook for 1–2 minutes. Spoon some sauce from the pan onto the top of the fish.

drinks
and
desserts

e and smoke
OCKTAIL

ve a spicy mezcal cocktail once in a while, and gochujang pairs well with the
noky, heady flavor of this Mexican spirit.

 **1 COCKTAIL**

INGREDIENTS

Salt and sugar for the rim
4 limes, cut into wedges
1 tsp gochujang, brought to room
    temperature
3/4 oz agave nectar (or simple syrup)
2 oz mezcal
4–5 cucumber slices

DIRECTIONS

For a salt/sugar rim, combine equal parts of
salt and sugar, wet the rim, and dip the glass
upside down into the mixture.

Squeeze the lime wedges into a cocktail
shaker, and then drop in the wedges.

Add the gochujang, agave, and mezcal, and
muddle together.

Add the cucumber slices and shake.

Pour into a rocks glass and garnish with
cucumber slices.

gochujang BLOODY MARY

I love everything about a Bloody Mary, from its tangy kick to its celery stick. This is a Korean-inspired take on this classic cocktail.

INGREDIENTS

2 tsp gochujang, at room temperature

4 oz tomato juice

1/2 lemon

2 oz vodka

2 oz soju (a clear distilled Korean liquor)

2 tsp prepared horseradish

1 dash Worcestershire sauce

1 pinch ground black pepper

1 pinch celery salt

Celery stalks for garnish

DIRECTIONS

Fill a tall glass with ice. Mix the gochujang and tomato juice together in a small bowl until it reaches an even consistency, and then set aside.

Give a good squeeze to the lemon so that the juice goes into a cocktail shaker. Add the vodka, soju, tomato-gochujang mixture, horseradish, Worcestershire sauce, pepper, and celery salt into the shaker. Fill the shaker with ice and shake gently.

Strain into glass and garnish with celery stalks.

hot and sweet
GINGER COCKTAIL

This sweet and spicy cocktail served in a martini glass has a snappy combination of flavors.

INGREDIENTS

1 tsp gochujang, brought to room temperature

2 oz ginger vodka

1 oz agave syrup

2 lime wedges, plus more for garnish

Sliced jalapeno pepper, seeded

Candied ginger (optional garnish)

DIRECTIONS

Muddle gochujang, vodka, and agave syrup in a shaker.

Squeeze juice of the lime wedges into the shaker, and then drop wedges in.

Add a couple jalapeno slices and ice.

Shake vigorously and strain into a martini glass.

Garnish with lime wedges or candied ginger.

spiced PEANUT COOKIES

Gochujang goes well with peanut butter and peanuts, so we sometimes make quick sesame noodles at home with a mixture of peanut butter, gochujang, and sesame oil. These cookies are the same idea in snack form, and they are delicious!

 ABOUT 40 COOKIES   **2 HOURS**

INGREDIENTS

1 1/2 cups unbleached all-purpose flour

1 tsp baking soda

1/2 tsp kosher salt

1/2 cup unsalted butter, at room temperature

2/3 cup brown sugar

1 large egg

1 tsp vanilla extract

3/4 cup creamy peanut butter

1/3 cup gochujang, at room temperature

1 cup chocolate chips

DIRECTIONS

In a large mixing bowl, mix together the flour, baking soda, and salt.

In another bowl or stand mixer, beat the butter and sugar together until light and fluffy. Add the egg and vanilla and beat on high. Add the peanut butter and gochujang, and then beat on a medium speed until combined. Scrape down the sides of bowl and add flour mixture on low speed. Mix until just combined. Remove dough and fold in the chocolate chips. Refrigerate dough for 1–2 hours to firm up.

Preheat oven to 325°F.

Line a pan or cookie sheet with parchment paper and roll pieces of the dough into 1-inch balls. Spread out on the cookie sheet and bake for 12–14 minutes. Remove from the oven and let cool. You will probably have to make 2 separate batches.

marble swirl cake
WITH A TWIST

A moist, delicious cake with a bit of mild spice, this recipe features a chocolate swirl made of Nutella, chocolate, and gochujang. The hazelnut, chili, and chocolate flavors make for a delicious combination.

 1 LOAF CAKE **1 HOUR 5 MINUTES**

INGREDIENTS

1 1/2 cups flour

2 tsp baking powder

3/4 tsp salt

1 cup sugar

1/4 cup plain Greek yogurt (full fat)

2 large eggs

1 tsp vanilla

1/4 cup butter

2 Tbsp agave nectar

1/4 cup vanilla almond milk

3 Tbsp semisweet chocolate chips

4 Tbsp Nutella

2 Tbsp gochujang

DIRECTIONS

Preheat your oven to 350°F. In a mixing bowl, mix the dry ingredients together—the flour, baking powder, salt, and sugar. In another mixing bowl, mix the wet ingredients together—the yogurt, eggs, vanilla, butter, agave, and almond milk. Incorporate the dry ingredients with the wet ingredients, mixing until it becomes a smooth batter.

Melt the chocolate chips in a double boiler or in the microwave at 50 percent power in 30-second intervals, stirring until it's melted. Pour 1/4 of the batter into another bowl and add in the melted chocolate, Nutella, and gochujang. Mix well to combine.

In a greased loaf pan, drop alternating spoonfuls of the vanilla and chocolate batter in a checkerboard pattern. Repeat another layer of the batter on top, dropping the vanilla batter on top of where you previously dropped chocolate, and vice versa.

With a wooden spoon, swirl the batters together by moving the spoon through in a crisscross and zigzag pattern. Don't overswirl the batters. Bake for 50 minutes. Remove and let sit on a cooling rack. Remove from pan after 10 minutes.

surprisingly spiced
FUDGE

This five-ingredient fudge recipe is simple, tasty, and has a surprising spicy kick.

 20 SERVINGS　 **15 MINUTES**

INGREDIENTS

1/2 cup dark chocolate chips

2 cups semi-sweet chocolate chips

1 (14-oz) can sweetened condensed milk

2 tsp vanilla

2 Tbsp gochujang

DIRECTIONS

In a double boiler or in a thick saucepan over low heat, combine the chocolate chips and sweetened condensed milk.

Mix and stir until the mixture is smooth, making sure it doesn't burn.

Add the vanilla and gochujang, and mix to combine well.

Pour into a greased 8-inch square pan and even out the top.

Chill in the fridge for a couple hours until firm.

Lift out of the pan and cut into squares.

If you are giving this as a gift or want some decoration, sprinkle the fudge with some coarse sea salt or some colored sugar.

acknowledgments

This book would not have been possible without a great idea from Kermit Hummel, the editorial director of Countryman Press. It's been a pleasure to work with such a visionary editor. I am also very thankful to managing editor Lisa Sacks, who oversaw the manuscript and kept me organized, and to copyeditor Diane Durrett for her meticulous eye.

Outside of the fine folks at Countryman, the most important person I have to thank is my husband, David, who was endlessly supportive. He took almost all the photos in this book and endured the waiting game of food photography. And I am always grateful for my sons, Lucas and Zeke, who make me smile and inspire me every day.

I have the deepest gratitude for the people who I have learned from over the years, but especially my grandmother and mother. They taught me to appreciate, love, and be open-minded to good food and cooking; they taught me the importance of sitting down and enjoying a communal meal. And I am continuously thankful for my sister, Helen, who has always been my best editor.

Thank you to all of my family and friends who, over the years, have cooked for me, have cooked with me, have shared meals with me, and in doing so have added to this book.

index